OBJECT ORIENTED PROGRAMMING

Demystified

COLIN GIRLING

Editing, design, typesetting and publishing by UK Book Publishing

www.ukbookpublishing.com

ISBN: 978-1-916572-41-6

OBJECT ORIENTED PROGRAMMING

Demystified

CONTENTS

CHAPTER 1:
INTRODUCTION TO OBJECT-ORIENTED PROGRAMMING

Prerequisites

This book is written for those who are familiar with a basic knowledge of procedural programming languages and who wish to learn object-oriented programming.

Some knowledge of programming and procedural programming languages, such as C or Pascal will be useful.

C will be used for procedural examples, with C++ and C# being used to provide object-oriented code examples. An in-depth knowledge of C, C++ or C# should not be required.

A subset of the Unified Modelling Language (UML) will also be used for the diagrams, but the notation of UML will be explained before the diagrams appear; therefore, no need for prior knowledge of UML will be required.

The C programming language is used early on to compare procedural programming against object-oriented programming, and most of the book will focus on C++ and C# object-oriented examples.

For C, C++ and C#, single line comments will use // and multi-line comments will use /* */ in code examples to improve readability.

The Goals for Better Software

Software generally grows in size over time as the products introduce more features; therefore, the larger the code becomes, the harder it is to keep the software organised and reliable.

Object-oriented programming helps solve some of the software organisational problems by allowing modelling of physical and conceptual paradigms with constructs such as encapsulation, inheritance and polymorphism, which will be explained later.

It is important to understand that object-oriented design and programming is just an approach to help manage software as it changes and grows whilst making it easier to re-use existing code, if it is done well.

Whatever software is produced it should aim to achieve the following:

Readability	Readable code is easier to understand and therefore easier to change.
	Keeping functions small and documenting them with comments can make it easier to understand.
	Review personal code to check if it still makes sense before delivery.
	Have others review the code to validate that it can be understood.
Simplicity	Finding the simplest solution to a problem will make it easier to understand the software and to change it later, as required.
Testability	Software should be testable, from a functional level up to the completed product.
	Automated tests that run after changes will help to ensure software is working as designed.
Reliability	The above points will help to achieve reliability, ensuring the product can survive the test of time whilst limiting any reputational damage for a product.

The Beginning of Object-Oriented Programming

Programming, before object-oriented design existed, was procedural and used variables and functions.

Programming languages such as Pascal or C are procedural languages and use functions, procedures and variables to implement software solutions.

As software grew, trying to manage all of these variables and functions became increasingly more difficult, so writing software to be re-usable became more of a challenge.

The C programming language is still widely used today with free and commercial software, such as Linux, still being written using C. However, writing large code bases in a procedural language takes a lot of care and discipline.

Those who worked with procedural programming languages realised, over time, that there were a lot of limitations and repetitive patterns of passing the same variables between many functions. This led programmers to try and implement better, re-usable code whilst still being constrained by the nature of the procedural language.

The C programming language has structures, and these could be used to group related variables together. This allowed them to be passed between functions as a whole, but the limitations of C meant the same pattern of passing these through many functions, making programming inefficient and laborious.

As more functions or methods are added with their variables, this leads to the relationship between them becoming more difficult to track or understand.

Attempts to improve the limitations of procedural programming led to the beginning of object-oriented programming and object-oriented languages such as Smalltalk, C++, C#, Java, Python, and others.

The Relationship Between Variables and Functions

Software is used to model real-life or logical problems and implement solutions with the use of programming languages.

Understanding the relationship between data and functionality is a fundamental element of improving how a programming language can model software.

In procedural programming languages this is done by defining functions that accept arguments that would be required to produce a result.

It might be necessary to have a function that can take a first and last name and then combine them with a space to separate them, as shown by function GetFullName on the next page.

Formally, the process of breaking down problems into their separate data and functional components is known as functional decomposition.

Firstly, observe a procedural example of the C programming language, assuming these functions are already implemented.

```
/* Define a function to add the first name and last name together,
      separated by a space, and return as a sequence of characters. */
char* GetFullName(const char* first_name,
                  const char* last_name);

// Work out the age in years from the birth date.
int GetAge(int day_of_birth, int month_of_birth, int year_of_birth);
```

This is how the functions would be used with variables:

```
// Create the sequence of characters for the first and last name.
char* first_name = strdup("John");
char* last_name = strdup("Smith");

int day_of_birth = 14;   // Day can be 1 to 31.
int month_of_birth = 4;  // Month can be 1 to 12.
int year_of_birth = 1975;

char* full_name = GetFullName(first_name, last_name);
int age = GetAge(day_of_birth,
                 month_of_birth,
                 year_of_birth);

printf("Name is %s and age %d\n", full_name, age);

free(first_name); // Characters need to be freed from memory.
free(last_name);
free(full_name);
```

In the C programming language, it is possible to define custom data structures.

When there is data using in-built types provided by the language like int or bool, these are known as variables.

When having data of a user defined structure or class (shown later), instances of these are known as objects.

With the use of a structure, there might be the following person structure and some functions to work with the structure, which can reduce how many arguments are used with the C functions.

```c
// Define the data structure for a person.
struct Person
{
  char* first_name;   // Sequence of characters for first name.
  char* last_name;    // Sequence of characters for last name.
  int day_of_birth;   // 1..31
  int month_of_birth; // 1..12
  int year_of_birth;  // e.g. 1975
};

char* GetFullName(const Person* p);
int GetAge(const Person* p);
```

This is how the functions would be used with this structure:

```c
// Create the object using the Person structure and set the values.
struct Person person;
person.first_name = strdup("John");
person.last_name = strdup("Smith");
person.day_of_birth = 14;
person.month_of_birth = 4;
person.year_of_birth = 1975;

char* full_name = GetFullName(&person);
int age = GetAge(&person);

printf("Name is %s and age %d\n", full_name, age);

/* Characters need to be freed from memory after
   their use is complete. */
free(person.first_name);
free(person.last_name);
free(full_name);
```

With an object-oriented language like C++, it is possible to define a class which allows variables and functions to be defined together, like this:

```cpp
// Define the data and functions for a person together.
class Person
{
  public:
    // Set the variables for the class when it is created.
    Person(std::string first_name,
           std::string last_name,
           int day_of_birth,
           int month_of_birth,
           int year_of_birth);

    std::string GetFullName() const;
    int GetAge() const;

  private:
    /* When the class variable is created, the variables
       will store the information about the person. */
    std::string m_first_name;
    std::string m_last_name;
    int m_day_of_birth;
    int m_month_of_birth;
    int m_year_of_birth;
};
```

This is how the class would be used:

```cpp
// Create the object using the Person class and set the values.
Person person("John", "Smith", 14, 4, 1975);

printf("Name is %s and age %d\n",
        person.GetFullName().c_str(),
        person.GetAge());
```

The string class provided by C++ also offers the ability to get the characters using the c_str function and display with the printf function, which can be seen in the above example.

CHAPTER 2:
THE CORE PRINCIPLES OF OBJECT-ORIENTED PROGRAMMING

Object-oriented programming comprises these core principles: abstraction, encapsulation, inheritance, and polymorphism, which are covered in subsequent chapters in more detail.

Abstraction

Abstraction is the process of identifying what is or is not important for the solution you wish to model and implement.

This should not be confused with abstract classes, which is detailed later and is part of polymorphism.

Encapsulation

Combining variables and functions or methods together within a class is how encapsulation is achieved, and is the most basic part of object-oriented programming.

Data hiding is used to restrict direct access to the variables from the outside world, which aids in providing robust encapsulated solutions.

The functional implementation is hidden, only exposing a publicly available set of functions or methods for the user.

Inheritance and polymorphism cannot be implemented without classes.

Inheritance

Functionality can be extended from existing classes by sharing functionality from existing classes and then by defining personal extensions.

Polymorphism

Existing behaviour from classes can be overridden to make them behave in different ways by using inheritance, thus overriding the behaviour of existing functions.

Other Considerations

Although generic programming is not considered to be part of object-oriented programming, it is often used to assist with abstraction, by making the data opaque.

Generic solutions can be designed and implemented without being concerned about the types of data.

CHAPTER 3:
ABSTRACTION

The beginning of any software system requires understanding of what will be modelled, which means identifying the high-level components of the system.

The components of a system would include any characteristic or behaviour that would reasonably be expected to be modelled.

Take the example of needing to develop a software solution for an elevator, where identifying that the elevator needs to travel to different floors and open or close the doors would need to be considered.

Looking at the high-level components of an elevator system, the elevator can be identified as a separate component that comprises doors, a control panel and maybe a need to model control over the motor that drives the elevator up and down.

There might also be a need to model an external control panel within the lobby to call for the elevator, or potentially call for one of multiple elevators.

Using the techniques of encapsulation, inheritance and polymorphism, the system can then be designed and implemented from the abstract parts of the system identified.

The scope of the system can also be considered early on, such as a limit on the number of floors, the number of elevators and other factors such as supporting negative floor numbers for basement levels.

CHAPTER 4: ENCAPSULATION

Going back to the earlier examples of the C and C++ code in the first chapter, the first difference to notice is that with the C++ code, the functions and the variables are all defined together within the class and protect the variables with data hiding.

The approach of combining the variables and functions is known as encapsulation and brings together all data and functionality that is related to each other, whilst hiding the details of the implementation.

Although defining the functions and variables together might seem like more work than the C alternative, once the class is defined it can be re-used many times, with less code required to handle the setup, clean-up, and less passing of variables into functions when using the class object.

A class can also access the variables defined within the class without the need to pass them as arguments to the functions, as the following C++ example shows:

```cpp
class Person
{
public:
  /* Set the first and last name at the time Person is created,
     within this function known as a constructor. */
  Person(std::string first_name,
         std::string last_name,
      ...)
    : m_first_name(first_name)
    , m_last_name(last_name)
  {
  }

  // Join the first and last names, separated by a space.
  std::string GetFullName() const
  {
    std::string full_name = m_first_name + " " + m_last_name;
    return full_name;
  }

private:
  std::string m_first_name;
  std::string m_last_name;
  ...
};
```

The above example of implementing a special kind of function that is known as a constructor, shows how it is automatically called every time a variable of the class Person is created.

Constructors have the same name as the class, which is what tells the compiler it is a constructor for C++ and C#, although this might not be true for all object-oriented languages.

The other function implemented is `GetFullName` which shows a simple example of adding two strings together.

Object-oriented languages provide classes already written for the users including `string`, which manages character sequences automatically and has features such as adding strings together.

Internally, the string class manages the memory for the sequence of characters for the users and handles all operations to change the allocated memory, or even re-allocate memory when the sequence of characters is too big to fit into the existing memory.

The `string` class is a simple but excellent example of good encapsulation, removing the need to manually allocate memory, re-allocate memory, or free the memory when the user is finished with it.

Furthermore, the string class provides a set of functions that allow the stored characters to be manipulated in various ways by the user, including indexing a character at a position, searching for a sequence of characters within a string variable, and more.

The above example not only demonstrates creating customised Person class, but also using an existing string class provided by C++ and C#, which demonstrates the advantages of having encapsulation and re-using existing code.

Why is data and functional hiding important?

For those familiar with procedural programming and specifically shared variables that many functions can be used to modify the shared variables, it becomes easy to change the variables' values and cause unexpected side effects.

Imagine if the `string` class had the variables as public, and variables `data` containing the characters and `length` were accessible by everyone?

The variable `data` would be easy for anyone to change without updating the variable `length`, potentially leaving the `data` and `length` variables in an invalid state.

Encapsulation allows access to data to be restricted externally with the use of private variables, and the integrity of the variables is maintained through an interface of the class, which provides a selection of functions or methods.

Hiding the implementation means that the internal workings do not need to be understood, or how the functionality interacts with the variables.

CHAPTER 5:
INHERITANCE

Object-oriented programming languages provide a feature known as inheritance, which allows a class to be re-used but also to add additional features to an existing class.

It is important to understand the difference between two concepts: "Is A" versus "Has A".

When something "Is A", then it can be used in a sentence in order to make sense, such as:

"A teacher **is a** person".

It would not be correct to say "A teacher has a person" because it would not make sense.

The same reasoning can be used for "Has A", such as:

"A person **has a** name".

Also, it would not be correct to say "A person is a name", because, again, it would not make sense.

Inheritance is exactly the same relationship as "Is A", and it is important to know that when using inheritance, the relationship needs to make sense.

Variables within a class provide the "Has A" relationship, so first name and last name are "Has A" relationship with the Person class defined earlier.

Languages such as C++ and C# provide the ability to inherit functionality from an existing class, and then to add in the new functionality to it, while still being able to share the existing functionality.

"Is A" vs "Has A" Examples

Supervisor **is a** person	Person **has a** weight
Square **is a shape**	Square **has a** size
House **is a building**	Building **has a** door
Car **is a vehicle**	Car **has an** engine
List **is a container**	List **has** items
Smartphone **is a device**	Device **has** power

The following C++ example shows how to define a `Teacher` class that inherits existing functionality from the existing `Person` class defined previously:

```cpp
// Teacher inherits from Person class defined previously.
class Teacher : public Person
{
public:
  Teacher(const char* first_name,
          const char* last_name,
          int day_of_birth,
          int month_of_birth,
          int year_of_birth,
          const char* subject)
    : Person(first_name,
             last_name,
             day_of_birth,
             month_of_birth,
             year_of_birth)
    , m_subject(subject)
  {
  }

  // Get the subject taught by the teacher.
  string GetSubject() const
  {
    return m_subject;
  }

private:
  std::string m_subject;
};
```

In the example above, the `Teacher` class is known as the derived class, child class or subclass, which extends the functionality of the `Person` class and adds a new variable `m_subject` to simulate what is taught.

The Person class is also described as a base class, superclass or parent class with this kind of relationship.

When a class inherits from another class, public functions such as GetFullName are visible from the derived Teacher class.

This would mean when there is a Person or Teacher object, both are able to use the GetFullName function, e.g.

```cpp
Teacher t("Bob", "Smith", 16, 02, 1970);
std::string full_name = t.GetFullName();
printf(full_name);
```

CHAPTER 6:
INTRODUCTION TO UNIFIED
MODELLING LANGUAGE (UML)

At this point it is worth introducing the readers to some basics of UML now that variables, functions, classes and inheritance have been covered, which will allow programmers to visually represent software.

A class is represented by a name within a box, and the blue colour will be used throughout. Member functions and variables can also be modelled as seen, with class name first. The functions and variables can be optionally shown within the box.

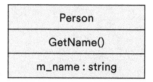

A line with an arrow represents inheritance of one class from another class.

A line with a filled diamond on the end shows ownership of a variable or object by a class. The class is responsible for ensuring the variable or object is cleaned-up or freed.

A line with an empty diamond shows a reference to a variable or object by a class, but the class is not responsible for managing the lifetime of the variable or object.

This is an example of class `Teacher` inheriting from class `Person`.

The class `Person` owns the lifetime of the `Clothes` object.

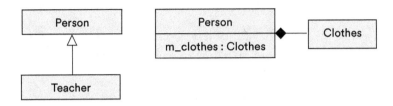

CHAPTER 7:
POLYMORPHISM

So far, encapsulation and inheritance have demonstrated how to combine data and functionality together, and also how to extend classes to provide further functionality.

One of the most important aspects of object-oriented programming is the ability to override the behaviour of functions in the base class from the derived classes.

Object oriented languages such as C++ and C# use the keyword `virtual` to allow a derived (or inherited) class to override the behaviour of base class functions.

The `override` keyword will cause the function within the derived class to be called instead of the base class, when the object is of the derived class type.

The following C# example demonstrates a practical use of overriding a virtual function:

```csharp
class Writer
{
  // Define WriteLines function to be implemented by derived classes.
  public virtual bool WriteLines(string[] lines)
  {
    return false;
  }
}

class ConsoleWriter : Writer
{
  public override bool WriteLines(string[] lines)
  {
    foreach (string line in lines)
      Console.WriteLine(line);
    return true;
  }
}

class FileWriter : Writer
{
  public FileWriter(string filename)
  {
    _filename = filename;
  }

  public override bool WriteLines(string[] lines)
  {
    System.IO.File.WriteAllLines(_filename, lines);
    return true;
  }

  private string _filename;
}
```

The above example shows how it is possible to have a generic Writer class, and how it can be customized to write to the console or a file.

With a small amount of code, it is possible to select the means of writing to the console or file, and it would take little more effort to allow a user, at some point in the future, to decide when they want to write to a console or a file.

```csharp
class Program
{
  // Select the writer needed for outputting the lines.
  private static Writer GetWriter(string filename)
  {
    if (String.IsNullOrEmpty(filename))
      return new ConsoleWriter();

    return new FileWriter(filename);
  }

  static void Main(string[] args)
  {
    string filename = "";

    try
    {
      Writer writer = GetWriter(filename);

      string[] lines = new string[] {
              "First line", "Second line" };

      if (!writer.WriteLines(lines))
        Console.WriteLine("No Writer is implemented!");
    }

    catch (System.ArgumentException e)
    {
      Console.WriteLine($"{e.Message}");
    }
  }
}
```

The first thing that can be noticed is that the Writer class is used for the generic writer object, but it is the ConsoleWriter and FileWriter that provide the implementation for the WriteLines function.

Polymorphism allows for the writer object to store a ConsoleWriter or a FileWriter object, and for the correct overridden WriteLines function to be used.

Although the class object is a Writer, the program knows when it is running, that the object is really a ConsoleWriter or FileWriter object, depending on what GetWriter returns to the writer object.

When the virtual keyword is used in the base class function and the derived classes override the base class function, the correct function will be used for the type of object.

This works because the language creates a look-up to the real object, which, in the previous example, is a ConsoleWriter or FileWriter. Once the correct class object is known, the language knows how to use overridden functions that are defined as virtual functions.

If the virtual and override keywords were removed, the function WriteLines on the Writer object would be used instead, because there would be no way to look up which function should be used.

Starting to think about polymorphism will lead to thinking about base classes with common functionality, which can later be implemented in derived classes.

The following UML can help to picture the relationships between the base and derived classes.

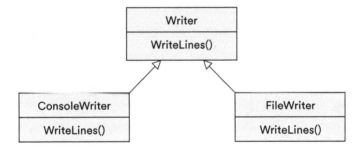

Take a look at the following two lines, and then some more information about how virtual functions work will be provided afterwards:

```
Writer writer = GetWriter(write_to_console, filename);
writer.WriteLines(lines);
```

Object-oriented language uses a virtual look-up table, also known as a vtable, that stores pointers to the correct functions that will be called.

The writer variable is of type Writer, but the vtable will point the WriteLines function for either the ConsoleWriter version or the FileWriter version, depending on which derived object is returned by GetWriter.

At run-time the correct function will be looked up and executed based on the vtable.

The following example will create a Writer object, and as the WriteLines function only returns false, nothing will happen and false will be returned.

The "not implemented" message will then be displayed.

```
Writer writer = new Writer();
string[] lines = {"line 1", "line 2"};
bool success = writer.WriteLines(lines);
if (!success)
   Console.WriteLine("WriteLines is not implemented");
```

This example demonstrates that the Writer object will have a vtable pointing to the ConsoleWriter virtual functions.

When the WriteLines function is called on this Writer object, the WriteLines function implemented by ConsoleWriter will be called.

The not implemented message will not be displayed, but line 1 and line 2 will be shown.

This is because the vtable for the Writer object now points to the ConsoleWriter vtable, and any virtual functions will use the ConsoleWriter implementation.

```
Writer writer = new ConsoleWriter();
string[] lines = {"line 1", "line 2"};
bool success = writer.WriteLines(lines);
if (!success)
   Console.WriteLine("WriteLines is not implemented");
```

CHAPTER 8:
INTERFACES AND ABSTRACT CLASSES

Interfaces have functions defined, but do not provide implementation for the interface; this is expected to be implemented by derived classes.

Abstract classes allow functions to be defined that provide implementation, but also allow functions to be defined that must be implemented from derived classes.

Be aware that later versions of C# allow implementation for interfaces, but this will not be covered or recommended, as abstract classes can achieve the same results.

Multiple interfaces can also be implemented by a class, allowing a single class to implement multiple interfaces.

The Writer class has a virtual function that can be overridden to change the function used when using derived classes, but if the `Writer` class was used without a derived class, `WriteLines` could still be used, even though it would do nothing except return false.

There is a way to force the `WriteLines` function to be overridden by derived classes so that the `Writer` class could not be used directly; this would prevent an object being created for a `Writer` class that served no purpose.

C# and C++ allow users to define interfaces forcing these functions to be implemented in the derived classes, and only usable by those derived classes.

Knowing that all functions within an interface must be implemented by derived classes allows the creation of generic solutions that only need to use the interface, therefore knowing that any derived class must implement any functions defined by the interface.

There is no need to have a `WriteLines` function that does nothing. What is needed is a way to force each class to implement functions that have real-life use.

This C# example shows how to change `Writer` to force the derived classes to implement the `WriteLines` function. Notice `Writer` was renamed to `IWriter` to indicate it is an interface:

```
interface IWriter
{
  // Define WriteLines function to be implemented by derived classes.
  bool WriteLines(string[] lines);
}
```

Changing the base class for `ConsoleWrite` and `FileWriter` from `Writer` to `IWriter` would guarantee that `WriteLines` must be implemented by derived classes.

This can be proven by removing `WriteLines` from `ConsoleWriter` or `FileWriter` and trying to compile the code, which would fail.

In C# using `interface` instead of `class` will automatically make the functions virtual without implementation, and derived classes do not need to use the `override` keyword, as this is already implied.

Abstract classes are similar to interfaces, with the exception that the class can have a mixture of implemented functions and functions that must be overridden; although it is still not possible to create an object for the abstract class directly, it must still be a derived class.

```
abstract class AbstractWriter
{
  // Define WriteLines function to be implemented by derived classes.
  public abstract bool WriteLines(string[] lines);

  // Implement a function to force any buffered writes to complete
  public virtual bool Flush() { return false; }
}
```

Notice that `Flush` defaults to returning `false`, as flush would be meaningless for writing to a screen.

Interfaces must implement the functions within derived classes.

Abstract classes must implement those functions not providing implementation in derived classes.

The `ConsoleWriter` class will implement the `WriteLines` function, not the `IWriter` interface.

It is, therefore, not possible to do this:

```
IWriter writer = new IWriter();
```

But it is possible to do this:

```
IWriter writer = new ConsoleWriter();
```

When `ConsoleWrite` has been derived from `AbstractWriter` then this would be the result:

```
AbstractWriter writer = new ConsoleWriter();
```

CHAPTER 9:
INVARIANTS

The relationship between variables and functions was previously discussed, but there is also an important relationship between different variables.

There are situations where the state of variables relating to each other must always be true, otherwise there could be a flaw in the system.

Unintentional flaws can exist within the system that do not cause any negative side effects. In order to avoid problems caused by these unintended flaws, meticulous system design should eradicate any accidental flaws, thereby ensuring the system does not fail or work unpredictably.

An invariant is a set of values and their conditions that are always expected to be true.

For example, the following code will expect the minimum values to be less or equal to the maximum value, otherwise there is a flaw in the software.

Hence, the minimum value being less or equal to the maximum value must always be true.

Let's consider the following example:

```
class MinMax
{
public:
  unsigned int GetRange() const
  {
    return m_max_value - m_min_value;
  }

  unsigned int m_min_value = 0;
  unsigned int m_max_value = 0;
};
```

The MinMax class is written with one important assumption: that the min value will always be less or equal to the max value, which can be determined by the use of unsigned types, meaning they cannot be negative numbers.

The function GetRange would return the incorrect value if min value was greater than max value.

Encapsulation allows programmers to enforce conditions that guarantee these flaws cannot be introduced, as the following example shows:

```cpp
class MinMax
{
public:
  unsigned int GetMinValue() const { return m_min_value; }
  unsigned int GetMaxValue() const { return m_max_value; }

  void SetMinValue(unsigned int min_value)
  {
    if (min_value > m_max_value)
      throw std::logic_error("Min value too big");
    m_min_value = min_value;
  }

  void SetMaxValue(unsigned int max_value)
  {
    if (max_value < m_min_value)
      throw std::logic_error("Max value too small");
    m_max_value = max_value;
  }

  unsigned int GetRange() const
  {
    return m_max_value - m_min_value;
  }

private:
  unsigned int m_min_value = 0;
  unsigned int m_max_value = 0;
};
```

By catching the error, at the earliest point, there is no need to check the min and max values before using them each time.

Alternatively, it is possible to return true or false for success or failure, for those systems that don't support exception handling.

CHAPTER 10:
TYPES

Programming languages provide primitive types that allow the user to create variables such as integers, floating point, boolean and characters.

Types describe the information stored, such as an integer storing a whole number, which can be signed or unsigned, and will use a fixed number of bytes in memory.

The C# type `uint` and the C++ type `uint32_t` stores an unsigned integer containing 32-bits of numerical information.

These types are built into the language, and procedural languages like C require the user to manage any types more complex than a simple character, integer or floating point themselves.

That means allocating, re-sizing and freeing character buffers for strings, etc.

Object-oriented languages like C++ and C# provide a string class as part of their library that does all of this work automatically and implements these functions efficiently.

The string class provides the ability to assign a value with =, add two strings together using +, and make it behave in a similar way to a basic primitive type, which makes it easier to use these objects like the string.

It is also possible to write customised classes and provide customised operators +, -, *, /, <, >, etc.

C++ and C# override operators slightly differently, and C++ can override = operator.

It is also possible to create other custom types by using classes, such as a list, array, etc.

The advantage of defining customised classes, which behave like types, is that it can make it easier to use them and to read them in a similar way to reading a primitive type.

Using += or < should be obvious in their meanings, e.g.

```
string s1 = "ab" + "cd";
string s2 = "ef" + "gh";
if (s1 < s2)
  Console.WriteLine($"{s1} is less than {s2}");
```

See the following C# example of how to implement a Writers class that allows 0 or more IWriter interfaces to be added to a list:

```
class Writers
{
  public Writers()
  {
    _writers = new List<IWriter>();
  }

  public void Add(IWriter writer)
  {
    _writers.Add(writer);
  }

  public void Add(List<IWriter> writers)
  {
    foreach (IWriter writer in writers)
      Add(writer);
  }

  public void WriteLines(string[] lines)
  {
    foreach (IWriter writer in _writers)
      writer.WriteLines(lines);
  }

  // Implementing + will automatically also add +=
  public static Writers operator +(Writers writers, IWriter writer)
  {
    Writers new_writers = new Writers();
    new_writers.Add(writers._writers);
    new_writers.Add(writer);
    return new_writers;
  }

  private List<IWriter> _writers;
}
```

Using the solution is as follows:

```
IWriter writer = GetWriter(filename);
string[] lines = new string[] { "First line",
"Second line" };
Writers writers = new Writers();
writers += writer;
writers.WriteLines(lines);
```

CHAPTER 11:
GENERIC PROGRAMMING

The previous examples show how to implement generic programming by providing a `WriteLines` function that can be overridden for the console and a file.

It is also possible to write generic software (not strictly part of object-oriented design) to work with types as well as functions, and the following C++ example shows how this can work:

```cpp
template<typename T>
class Calculator
{
public:
  // Initialise m_total to the default value, which is 0 for numeric.
  Calculator() : m_total()
  {
  }

  // Sum will add the values to the existing value of total and
  // return the new total.
  const T& Sum(const list<T>& values)
  {
    for (T value : values)
      m_total += value;
    return m_total;
  }

private:
  T m_total;
};
```

The above example shows how any type that provides += can be used to create a sum from a list of values.

Notice that if the type is numerical, such as an int or double, all the values would be added together and provide the sum of all the values.

If the type was a string, then all the values would be appended and a long string would be returned.

Using the above Sum function for different types is as simple as this:

```
list<int> int_values{ 1, 2, 3 };
list<string> str_values{ "A", "B", "C" };
Calculator<int> c1;
Calculator<string> c2;
printf("%d\n", c1.Sum(int_values));
printf("%s\n", c2.Sum(str_values).c_str());
```

CHAPTER 12:
SOFTWARE DESIGN PROBLEMS

Good software design is an attempt to limit the number of problems that are introduced into a software system, whilst also attempting to produce software that can continue to be developed and maintained over time.

Understanding how to identify these problems early, and how to either resolve them or keep on top of problems becoming worse, is discussed in relation to technical debt and refactoring next.

It is important to have a testing strategy that can continuously verify the system is working as expected.

Technical Debt

Any identified problems within a software system are considered technical debt.

Here are some common technical debt issues:

+ Bugs are when software is not behaving as expected, and is the most common type of technical debt, although not every bug in software will be serious enough to be a problem for users.

+ Duplicate code, which has been copied from somewhere else, increases the chances of software failures in the future and the code should be placed in a common, re-usable place. Often, problems may later be found in the software, and duplicate code is difficult to locate, resulting in problems being resolved in one copy, but missed in others.

+ When the performance is not acceptable, this can gradually become worse as changes to the software are made, or the inputs to the system, such as data from a database, are not carefully managed. Identifying what parts of a system need to perform well early on can reduce or eliminate the gradual degradation in performance over time.

+ When a change seems to be bigger than expected, this can sometimes be an indicator that the design of the software has problems. Overly complex designs can lead to increasing the time and effort required to make future changes.

+ Unused code can become stale and no longer functioning as originally designed and should be removed.

CHAPTER 13:
REFACTORING

The need to change software without affecting the existing behaviour of the system is described as refactoring.

It is important to test the software, before and after the refactoring, to ensure the behaviour is identical.

The behaviour of the software about to be changed should be fully understood before changes are made.

Considerations before refactoring software should include the following:

+ Readability needs improving because the software is becoming difficult to understand. Keeping software clean and readable will reduce errors when changes are made, and will also save time making future changes. If a piece of code has been identified as difficult to maintain and is changing frequently enough to cause problems, refactoring can be used to ensure future changes are more reliable.

+ There are frequent bugs in the software, caused by the fragile nature of the existing design or implementation, and refactoring can often make software more robust, meaning changes are required less often. A reduction in changes means less maintenance costs and more time to develop the software features.

+ There is a need to implement new features and it has been identified that refactoring can improve re-usability of the existing software. To eliminate the copying of existing code, thereby making software re-usable, which will save time when implementing new features and also makes it easier to test common components.

+ Obsolete code needs removing so cleaning up software will save engineering time, because people can often waste time trying to identify whether or not code is required.

- Performance needs improving and sometimes refactoring is required, but there needs to be awareness that performance can affect a system's behaviour, especially when multi-threaded, or when the software has some time-dependent side effect. It is important that software can be changed and performance improved without introducing unexpected side effects, and this should be considered when developing a system.

CHAPTER 14:
NAMING

The naming of classes, functions, variables and types is one of the most important aspects of encouraging good software practices and aids in better design, as well as making code easier to understand because it provides context.

In real life there are conversations held at a level where everyone can understand what each person is discussing, therefore communication is an important factor in both life and software naming.

The names used for classes, functions, variables and types will generally remain unchanged, once the initial implementation is complete, and it is the most important factor in helping to make the source code readable.

Consequently, poor naming will have the opposite effect, making it harder to understand what the software is doing. This adds extra time when changes are required later by someone who is unfamiliar with the software.

Keep the names as simple as possible as this will allow more people to understand what they are reading, therefore making it easier for more people to modify later on.

Good naming will also help to provide the context between classes, functions, types and variables.

Consider the following classes, Vehicle, Car and Engine. The relationship between them should be fairly obvious from the naming used.

Clearly, from the naming alone, it should be easy to see Car is inherited from Vehicle, and the Vehicle base class has an Engine object.

Function naming should be descriptive, and avoid using the class name as part of the function naming, for example for the Car class, there might be a function named StartEngine, or the Engine class might have the function Start.

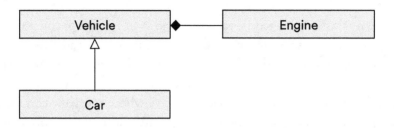

CHAPTER 15:
COUPLING

When any piece of code uses another piece of code, it becomes a coupling.

Sometimes coupling cannot be avoided; in fact, sometimes it is desirable and required, but a coupling should only be introduced when absolutely necessary.

When changing code, any coupling risks changing, or breaking, the behaviour of the design.

In the earlier example, `ConsoleWriter` and `FileWriter` classes were inherited from `IWriter` class, and so these are a direct coupling. Changing `IWriter` will most likely cause `ConsoleWriter` and `FileWriter` to be changed, especially if modifying existing functions within the interface.

Furthermore, it can be seen that changing `ConsoleWriter` will not affect `FileWriter`.

The existing design provides a separate way to output to the console, or to a file. The design has been deliberately created in this way to prevent file or console output from being affected by either one being changed.

There may be a need to output to the console and a file, thus it is possible to add a `ConsoleFileWriter` class that could use `ConsoleWriter` and `FileWriter`.

This design will allow any problems fixed with the `FileWriter` class to also be shared with `ConsoleFileWriter` class.

Every design should focus on ensuring that there is minimal coupling in order to minimise unwanted side effects, when a change is made.

Reducing coupling means that objects can be freed earlier, because long-term references to other objects do not need to be retained.

Techniques such as adding abstraction or using event systems, provided by the object-oriented languages, can be used to remove direct coupling.

Circular References

A specific problem with coupling is that, when object A references object B, and object B references object C, and object C references object A, it creates what is known as a circular reference.

The tightest form of a circular reference is a bi-directional reference, when object A references object B and object B references object A.

These couplings in a software system cause problems, and should be avoided unless they are absolutely necessary.

The following problems can be experienced with circular references, including bi-directional references:

- For languages such as C++ where resources are manually managed, freeing an object in a circular reference introduces the chance of other objects referencing an object that no longer exists.

- Where garbage collection languages such as C# are used, objects will not be freed until all coupling has been identified as no longer used. Circular referenced objects will only be freed once all of them are no longer required.

- If there is a need to release an object early because some resource, such as a file handle, needs to be closed as part of the freeing process, this may not be possible with existing circular references, or if handles are held open longer than desired.

- When there are circular references, any change to one part of the chain of references can affect the behaviour of other parts of the chain, and each one of the items in the chain will probably need to be compiled each time any one item is changed.

- Circular references in components or libraries can force unwanted changes to be implemented, allowing components to be compiled without a dependency being compiled first If two components were both dependent on each other, it would be impossible to build one without the other and would require undesirable changes to circumvent the problem.

A simple way to remove a bi-directional coupling would be to implement a third class.

The two classes that were bi-directionally coupled would then interact only through the third class.

A common example of this type of problem can be demonstrated with a `Person` and `Property` class.

Often, the mistake would be to have a `Person` class have a reference to the `Property` object and a `Property` class have a reference to the `Person` object, meaning changing one class will introduce risk to the other.

By considering the context of the new class within the system, the classes would be separated with another class, such as a `Record` class, which then has a reference to `Person` and `Property` objects and offers a suitable interface.

CHAPTER 16:
COHESION

Cohesion is described as a state where a group is united or objects stick together, and for object-oriented programming, the cohesion is managed at the class level by focusing on what each class models.

In terms of object-oriented design, only something that is directly related to the problem being solved should be part of the solution, whether that is a whole system, component, class, or function.

When considering the design of a class, focus on the following points:

+ Do the methods on a class have a meaningful relationship to the class?

+ Can the solution be re-used without needing to work around an existing behavioural problem for the existing solution?

+ Does the solution need to be changed to make it re-usable?

+ Is the solution extensible without breaking the existing solution?

Challenge the design, try to break it and see if it survives.

Ask questions about the design; does this decision belong here?

Will a change elsewhere break the design unexpectedly?

Here are some examples to help identify where cohesion might work and fail:

+ When defining a `Person` class, adding properties like first name and last name would be suitable options. It might be tempting to add age, but it would be better to use the birth date, allowing for the accurate age to be calculated.

+ Although people live somewhere, avoid adding information to a `Person` class such as an address, as it's not directly associated to a person. What happens if the address changes or the property is knocked down? Suddenly the information is wrong about the person.

+ A `File` class would not output anything to the screen, as this would make it impossible to perform file operations without altering the display.

Cohesion aims to offer a robust design that can be used without introducing unexpected side effects when reasonable changes are required.

CHAPTER 17:
ELEMENTS OF OBJECT-
ORIENTED PROGRAMMING

Identifying the components of a system

Object-oriented programming takes real-life or theoretical problems, or a combination of both, and produces software that will solve these problems.

Before starting to develop a system, there will be a need to define the scope of the system and identify all the components of the system.

These components can then be broken into smaller parts; this will give the functionality and properties that the components will provide.

When deciding on what functionality is going to be provided for the components, consider what the user of the components would most likely expect to be available and list them.

Remember to keep all components decoupled as this will make it much easier to develop and test them, without needing to worry about breaking other components of a system.

Decoupling of any system should be considered early on because removing high coupling is more time consuming than when introducing them. (See Refactoring)

Identifying object-oriented elements

When dealing with problems, it is important to identify all the elements that the software system will be implementing.

Early design will consider the interfaces and classes that are required within the system, as well as the class hierarchies one might expect to see as part of the design.

It should be expected that, as the design and implementation proceeds, some of these decisions will be changed.

Try to test design construction early on so that any problems with the design can be changed promptly.

Generally, as a system is implemented, design becomes harder to change as the system grows. There may come a time when it becomes necessary to work around design problems instead of re-designing those parts of the system.

There must be a willingness to accept that problems exist and to change them at the earliest opportunity, otherwise this will add an additional burden to all

those working on a system as it continues to change in the future.

Polymorphism, interfaces and generic programming

Each approach to solving design problems comes with positives and negatives; although sometimes there is an obvious choice to be made, occasionally, experimenting may also be required to make the best design decisions.

When considering which approach to use, some options are available that help to decide the one that is best for the problem being solved.

Design decisions need to be made based on readability, and extensibility, thus keeping complexity to a minimum. Performance should also be considered (but not at the cost of worsening readability).

When to use polymorphism

This approach has many advantages over generic programming because it offers context in readable code, when done well.

Having context when reading code means code is usually easier to read and understand.

Because polymorphism models real physical or conceptually recognised elements, the context is free with the good naming.

So, if there is a base class named Creature, and a derived class named Human, it can be seen by the naming and inheritance that it is engaging with some extendable system that is dealing with creatures, and that humans are an extension of the `Creature` class.

Modelling many things in this way allows the solutions to be put together in a manner that is likely to remain consistent for a long time without the need to make many changes.

Then it becomes fairly easy, and quick, to identify properties that are for all creatures, such as birth date, sex, number of limbs, weight, etc.

Identifying attributes that are specific to a human, and not a generic property of a creature, can then be determined, such as spoken languages, careers, etc.

Good design of classes means that, usually, once the properties have been identified, they will not need to be changed. There is always the opportunity to update classes later with extra properties.

Situations where physical or theoretical problems generally remain consistent through time are well suited to using traditional object-oriented design and polymorphism.

A common, telling sign that polymorphism is required is when there are lots of `if` or `switch` statements being used.

One example of how to identify whether to use polymorphism is when there is a `Circle` and `Square` class and code exists to check the type of shape before drawing.

Here is an example of not using a polymorphic solution:

```
void RefreshDocument(Circle circle, Square square)
{
    string shape_type;
    ...
    // Draw parts of the document.
    ...
    if (shape_type == "circle") circle.Draw();
    else if (shape_type == "square") square.Draw();
}
```

The polymorphic solution would have a Shape class with a virtual function called Draw, and each derived class would implement their own Draw functions.

Here is an example of using a polymorphic solution:

```
void RefreshDocument(Shape* shape)
{
    ...
    // Draw parts of the document.
    ...
    shape->Draw();
}
```

When to use interfaces

When a common pattern can be identified, but part of that implementation needs to be dynamically changed at runtime, then interfaces are a good way to solve these types of problems. (*See Polymorphism*)

One simple example of where the interface approach might work well would be with a file reader and writer.

If there was a need to read data from text files and binary files, an interface such as IFile could define functions Open, Read, Write, Append, Size, Close, etc.

The interface would define the parameters that should be met by the derived classes implementing the interface, such as the Read function reading the entire file contents and returning the contents within a string.

Here is an example of what the `IFile` interface might look like:

```
class IFile
{
public:
  IFile() {}
  virtual ~IFile() {}
  virtual void Open(string filename, string mode) = 0;
  virtual string Read() = 0;
  virtual void Write(string data) = 0;
  virtual void Append(string data) = 0;
  virtual unsigned long Size() const = 0;
  virtual void Close() = 0;
};
```

Then `TextFile` and `BinaryFile` classes could be implemented with the differences required between text and binary files, but with a common set of functions available through the `IFile` interface.

The `IFile` object would then be used to handle text or binary files using the same functions, as the following example demonstrates:

```
IFile* f = new TextFile();
f->Open("test.txt", "w");
f->Write("Some example text");
f->Close();
```

There is no need to share a `TextFile` or `BinaryFile` object with other functions or objects, but instead share the `IFile` object while knowing the interface is common between all file handling objects.

Here is a partial example of what the `TextFile` class implementation might look like:

```
class TextFile : public IFile
{
public:
  void Open(string filename, string mode) override
  {
    m_file_handle = fopen(filename.c_str(), mode.c_str());
  }

  string Read() override
  {
    string buf;
    int ch;
    if (!m_file_handle)
      return buf;
    fseek(m_file_handle, 0, SEEK_SET);
    while ((ch = fgetc(f)) != EOL)
      buf.push_back((char)ch);
    return buf;
  }

private:
  FILE* m_file_handle = nullptr;
};
```

The `Open`, `Read`, `Write`, `Append`, `Size` and `Close` functions would use different types of file handles and internally different functions for text and binary files, depending on the platform or operating system being targeted.

When designing interfaces, it is worth considering differences in platforms and hiding platform specific details within the implementation of each derived class, such as within `TextFile` or `BinaryFile`.

This would allow for an interface such as `IFile` to be used without concerning the users with needing to manually detect the platforms, as can be seen in the earlier example of using the `IFile` object.

When to use generic programming

Generic programming is suited to situations where the interface is always the same, but the type of data is going to be different.

If there was a need to have a common set of functions that conceptually do the same thing for many different types, then generic programming is ideal.

One example of this might be having a `Calculator` class, that will work with integer and floating-point types.

We know conceptually that functions `Add`, `Subtract`, `Multiply` and `Divide` will all be consistent in each of their individual operations, although the implementation for each type might have a different implementation.

Clearly, adding two 32-bit integers of value 1 and 2 is going to return 3; likewise, adding two 64-bit integers of 1 and 2 will also return 3, or float type, etc.

Thinking about design independently

Design usually changes the least within software, unless there is a serious enough problem within software that the changes need to be re-worked or replaced entirely.

It is important that design is given enough time to be considered, but also people with design experience should be engaged in any new design, to ensure there is a review process early on in order to avoid potential problems.

When considering any design, think about what has already been described previously in this book, but also appreciate that working with existing software might not solve problems satisfactorily.

Technical debt will exist, but there may also be a bigger problem with the people working on existing software just following a pattern or approach they have been used to for a long time, without considering the consequences of the additional technical debt being introduced.

Although design patterns will not be covered in this book, it is important to question if patterns are solving a problem in a way that makes the software easier to maintain, or adding unnecessary complexity that could be solved in a different way.

It is always important to ensure software design is being done for reasons described throughout the book, and not because a pattern is in fashion, or someone wishes to learn a new pattern and use it, ignoring the consequences of its use within the software.

ACKNOWLEDGEMENTS

Thank you to my wife Amabelle Girling for supporting me while I wrote the book.

Thank you goes to my mother Pauline Barnatt for reviewing the grammar.

I wish to say a thank you to the following people who reviewed the technical content of the book

+ Robert Pollard

+ Nil Karadağ

+ Mark Winter

+ Bilge Şenol